101

Questions to Improve Your Novel

for Writing, Editing, Revising, and Polishing

Kristen James

Author of

Blockbuster Books, Broken Down:
Learn from Bestselling Novels to Build Your Own
(Plotting with the novel map)

and

Authorpreneur:
Making Steady Income from ebook Royalties

ISBN 978-0692448717

AUTHORPRENEUR PRESS

First Edition

The following guide is the author's observations and insights, and is offered to help authors with writing and revising a novel.

Kristen James has over thirty published works which have hit the top 100 in Kindle in the US, UK, and Canada. A few of her fiction titles include *Point Hope, More Than Memories,* and *All In My Head.* Her nonfiction includes *Authorpreneur, How to be a Full Time Writer,* and *Blockbuster Books, Broken Down.*

www.writerkristenjames.com/nonfiction

101

Questions

to

Improve Your Novel

Contents

Hello There...

Do you love storytelling and writing? Do you have a burning desire to improve your craft? If you're like me, I bet you enjoy finding new writing techniques or understanding an element of story and structure in a new way. Writing a novel can be incredibly exciting and hard at the same time. You should celebrate when you complete a manuscript! And then buckle down for the editing and revising process, which can also be fun and rewarding because you have the words down on the page and now you get to make your story shine.

Most writers enjoy working on their finished draft. That's when it really comes together; it's like putting the finishing touches on a house. At the same time, all authors, from unpublished to beginning to bestselling, feel nervous that the next book won't be up to par. You're not alone in that. All of us felt that way about our first novel, and bestselling authors feel it about their new releases too. It's a constant game of, "Will they like it?" It's tough! I know. And I'd like to make it easier for you.

That's the idea behind this book: I thought, what if we could have a checklist to help us polish a novel? I've been working on my own list for the last few years, and now I'm sharing it with you. Not all questions will apply to every story or genre, and some lean toward my opinion on writing, but it's my aim for most of these questions and tips to guide you in evaluating and improving your work. I hope this book will be a rich resource for you in the editing and revising process, and help you enjoy it even more.

Wishing you the very best in your writing journey,
Kristen James

All About Story

On the web, content trumps all. In fiction, story is king. So I'd like to share a blog post I wrote about the power of story.

A story and a sentence walked into a bar together...

They both noticed a woman with long, dark hair and an inviting smile, so they sat at the bar, four stools away from her. She glanced over at their entrance before turning back to her conversation with her friends. Sentence told Story, "Watch this. I'm going to wiggle my perfect construction at her. She won't be able to resist!"

Story watched as Sentence tried to catch the woman's eye. The woman and her friends gave Sentence a few polite glances, but they weren't interested.

When Story had enough, he announced, "My turn!" He walked around Sentence to sit closer to the woman and gave her a nod and a wink. The woman immediately moved down the bar three seats to talk to Story.

"Your characters are amazing! How did you come up with this idea, anyway?" She leaned closer and tilted her head back to tease him with a half smile. "And the twist at the end! I didn't see that coming, but then it made perfect sense. Please tell me there's a sequel. Does Jake ever win Kathryn over, and does his father ever forgive him? Is there another mystery to solve?"

Story motioned for another round of drinks and murmured, "I'll tell you everything if you have a few hours..."

Sentence sulked in his seat. What had he done wrong?

"Sentence" missed the simple fact that readers don't go into bookstores and online retailers to buy groups of sentences. There aren't any reviews that read, "This book is full of perfect sentences! Check out the metaphor on page 82. The sentences were so wonderful that I forgot about the story and highlighted the commas and semicolons. This author knows how to vary sentence length! Wonderful!"

Readers often say a novel is well written, and they might mention the imagery or fresh use of language, but that alone won't win readers. Personally, I don't want to throw a reader out of the story with an impressive sentence. I want the plot and characters to pull the reader in so she'll keep reading past her bedtime. Of course, I don't want poor writing to distract the reader either, but I know the point of the novel is the story.

As an artist, do you want others to see the picture you're painting or the brushstrokes?

Do you need to write well on a sentence level to write good stories? Yes, of course! But are the sentences more important than the story you're telling? Not in my opinion. Aren't authors selling *stories*, not sentences?

Writing well is very important. I don't mean to argue that point, but it really bothers me when I hear someone put down a mega bestselling author for their writing. It's usually on a sentence level: "Look at all the clichés, passive voice, and simple sentences! A fifth grader could write better." It could be true–the given book might very well be full of sentences that could be written better. Maybe their modifiers don't line up. Maybe they like using clichés as shortcuts in certain places. Maybe they choose choppy or run on sentences over proper grammar to show the character's thoughts and emotions. But, if the writing really is that poor, then the author must be doing something else right. And that "something else" really sells copies. Millions of readers are buying those books. Despite what people say, you can't sell a book month after month on marketing alone. If it's not a good story, people complain. They won't tell other people about the book.

Readers want an experience away from their life. They want to get sucked into a great story that makes them forget everything else for a few hours. They want to connect with the character and see the world differently. They want to experience a great story. They want to *feel*.

So, yes, please learn to write sentences well and play with language. Study English, spelling, and grammar. Create fresh images and strive to be original. Learn how to write well so readers can understand what you're saying. And if you want to sell that writing, remember your job is to tell a damn good story.

*****

We can learn from every novel we read, even if we feel it could be improved. If it's reaching readers and selling, what did the author do right? My brother-in-law recently told me that one of the best books he's read in a while was horribly written. "The story was so great, I couldn't put it down despite that." Of course, we want quality writing that is free of typos and errors, but it'll benefit us as writers to realize perfect writing won't sell a bad or boring story. Accordingly, this book focuses on improving story along with writing.

All About Editing

I run into confusion about editing all the time, even when working with editors and proofreaders. Authors aren't always aware of the different kinds of editing, either. So here is an overview of the production process, including editing and proofreading, in the usual order. (Although sometimes you complete a step and go back to editing.)

Most writers edit and revise their first draft before sharing it, although some find it useful to get help before revising too much, especially if it's their first or second book. There is some debate on whether you should edit while writing or complete a draft before going back over things. Personally, I like to write a scene and then go through it several times, but I keep moving and adding new scenes every day too. I think it's most helpful to wait until you have a full manuscript before doing heavy editing, rewriting, and revising, unless you find a big issue while writing that needs to be addressed.

Self editing is all the work you do on your own, such as using this book, to evaluate your manuscript. Self editing includes looking at the story and writing, along with line editing and even proofreading. We should strive to make our work the best it in can be at every step and level, and then have others work on it as well.

Beta readers can be professionals, members of a book club, or friends who read your type of story. For the best results, they should read a lot and have experience discussing novels. Some beta readers can only tell you if they liked the story or not, or if it "worked." Others can point out strong and weak places, or even elements that need work. Many authors have their "first reader" who will be hard on the book and work to make it even better. I ask my beta readers to be as harsh as possible. I'd rather hear it from them than an Amazon reviewer! I might not always take their advice, but it's valuable feedback to see how they react and what they say. My first reader is usually my husband, who will tell me honestly if a scene isn't working, the character is acting out of character, a sentence is awkward, or a plot point just doesn't work for him. He's not a romance reader so he can see the story more objectively. This works really well for me, but some authors will tell you their spouse is the last person they want offering feedback. It all depends on what kind of reader they are.

You can find beta readers through your writing group, Facebook groups and friends, and friends and family if you can trust their feedback to not be biased. You can also hire freelancers to do a critique through a site like www.elance.com. (Which is in the process of merging with Odesk to become to www.upwork.com in 2015.)

A **story edit** is a deep or heavy edit that looks at construction, plot and character development, and the big writing issues. This can be a detailed critique or even working with a "book doctor." Many professional editors offer both a story and then a line edit, and some combine these to give feedback on the story while performing a line edit. I edit several novels a year, and I use Word's comment feature to point out and explain issues along with possible solutions, and I'll explain my edit if I think it's not clear. Sometimes I'll mark chapters or sections that need so much work they're not ready for a line edit. If you end up rewriting parts, or the story needs a lot of work, it's a good idea to have a separate story and line edit. Some authors have me do a story and line edit, and then have another editor go through for just line editing. More feedback and more eyes will catch more things.

The **line edit** looks at smoothing out sentences, and maybe some bigger issues such as paragraph placement and length, story details, and the flow. My line edits always contain a few comments because I want to offer all the feedback I can.

The final **proofread** should be focused on catching typos, misspelled words, missing words, wrong words, spacing issues, and grammar.

You should also conduct your own **final read through,** and even have a few readers go through the book. There are readers online that state on their blog, website, or Facebook that they love to beta read for authors. These are often different from an early "beta reader" that gives in depth feedback—these often will simply point out any last typos that got through the process.

The Beginning

The beginning can feel like a giant mountain that you must climb to get to the rest of the story. How do you craft the perfect opening that will pull readers in? For me, it's all about the character's voice and the promise of story. When you begin a new novel, I humbly suggest that you simply start with the first scene where something happens, and get going with the story. You can revise later, add to, or cut later on. This method keeps you from getting stuck at the beginning so you can finish that draft.

If you have a draft, these questions will help you consider if you started in the best place and in the best possible way for your story.

Quick note: I use "hero" to include hero, heroine, or even main character.

1. Did you accidentally start with one of the big no-nos?

Such as:
- Waking to the alarm clock
- Describing the weather
- The character is alone, thinking
- The character is going about their normal day
- A battle or action scene that isn't related to the story
- A battle or action scene, period, can be bad because we don't know the characters yet
- Character running into a crime scene (it's been overdone)

- False beginning: a dream, vision, flashback or anything that is only there to trick us into reading more, but isn't a natural part of the story
- Prologues (most of the time)
- Long character description (stick for a few traits to start)

Is there any way to cut this and start with your character doing something? If you've used one of the big no-nos, do you have good reason, and does it really work? Check with beta readers who read your genre to see if they would keep reading.

Some of you might have thought of novels that successfully used one of the above openings. They do work sometimes, but it's a gamble. Some openings on the list have been used so much that people groan when they see them.

2. Does your novel start with something happening?

This sounds pretty obvious, right? But take a second look. The opening is such a complicated matter that sometimes we get it all wrong without realizing it. I've started writing novels and later realized nothing really happened on the first page; I was merely getting to know my characters and story. "Happening" does not have to mean a big, flashy event, either. For a fun exercise, go to your bookshelf or Kindle, and read the opening scene in several of your favorite novels. Can you identify what pulls you into the story in each one?

There are many ways to start a novel, but one strong way to have something *happening*—not *going to* happen.

3. Does your novel start with conflict?

This can be a big conflict, or sizzling under the surface, or even something subtle, but it needs to be there. Maybe you simply need to add some discontent into your hero's life, or show an unspoken conflict with the other person in the opening. It's amazing how much conflict and tension you can add with a few hints, double meanings, body language, thoughts, and even tone of voice. Most communication isn't verbal. Use everything!

At the end of this section I share three of my novel openings to illustrate how to jump right into the story. These openings also have built-in conflict, although it's not a shouting match in any of them. Strong conflict doesn't have to be yelling, bullets flying, or a life in the balance. Stories can open that way, but readers connect to personal, inner struggles because they identify with them.

In Plot and Structure, I supply a novel diagram that shows a Big Bang event close to the novel's opening, defined as something that shatters or changes the hero's life.

4. Does your opening make people wonder what will happen next?

Of course, it's a little hard to tell that on your end as the author, but take a look at your first scene. Does it raise questions that will propel readers to the second scene? These "questions" can be:

- What happens next?
- Why did he do that?
- What caused that to happen?
- What will the hero do about that?
- Why is she feeling that way?
- What will she do about this feeling of unease?

If you find your opening lacking a story question, can you add one in with a few hints of the opening conflict? The "question" might also be a promise. The first scene shows something is off, or about to happen, or building momentum, and the reader wants to see how this first event or inner struggle will play out. As you edit and revise your early chapters, think of what kind of bread crumb trail you're leaving for readers.

5. Does your story start with an event that affects the hero?

Sometimes it works to build up to meeting the main character, but be careful with that method! The biggest thing that pulls readers in is the narrative voice of the character. We want to meet the person at the core of the story. So the opening pages and big events should affect the hero. If your novel's opening scene and/or first chapter don't involve the hero, do the events change the hero's life? And related to that…

6. Do you begin your novel with a character that isn't a main character?

This might not be a problem. It works in mystery and thrillers when it's a crime or important event, and often the character isn't named for plot reasons. However, if you're not writing a mystery or a thriller, be careful about doing this. Do you have a very good reason? Could you move this scene so that the book opens with your main character? Remember that readers often preview a book before committing. The opening is critical for reader connection.

7. Are things going well or okay in the first chapter? Is your main character happy?

This is also known as a boring opening. A novel exists because things are changing. It's the story of how the given change affects the hero, thus providing us with insights into how we can react to life.

I know you've heard over and over again to create a hero people will connect with, respect, admire, and want to be. However, creating a nice, good, happy character won't make readers connect. We don't want to read about a happy person with a good life because that won't show us anything. We read to escape and see how other people live their lives— our brain is actually researching how to survive and thrive in various situations. Give your hero an admirable trait, but flaws too. We bond with characters that feel a need to change in some way.

The biggest issue with the "happy hero in a nice world" is the lack of conflict and impending doom. If your opening lacks conflict, can you add a sense of unease, unrest, doubt, confusion, guilt, or even an expectation of impending change? How about just a sense of a coming storm, or that things aren't as they seem? This is that extra touch that makes readers wonder what will happen and how you'll resolve this unease.

Little changes make a big difference, so don't pound this into the ground. Just a few thoughts can add this unease. You can even create it through the way the character sees the setting. Here are two examples:

The thick clouds and pouring rain washed the world away in gray; the buildings outside were slipping away just like the rest of her life.

He climbed out of the car, and the bright sunshine and new, vibrant green leaves on the maples made Josh feel like he was getting a fresh start. As he took in the old farm house, the front door opened. Andrew bounced down the steps and flashed a beaming smile as he extended his hand in greeting. Could things be okay? But how could it all work out when he knew what they were doing here?

8. What is the reason your story starts where it does?

If you begin telling your story before anything changed, can you move your opening up? In the past, authors used a lot of set up. These days it's more common to start the novel after something has happened, such as a disaster, murder, bad news, or even good news that changed things for your hero.

Did you simply start the story in the morning when your character wakes up? How can you change that? Why not start the story later in the day, when the big inciting incident happens? I like to start my novels right when things change. There are other ways that work very well too, just as long as you have some kind of tension and something to make readers curious about the story.

9. Do you start the story as late as possible?

Consider jumping in "mid stream," after things have started to change. Just be careful that you don't have to then explain back story.

If you can cut your first scene or the first few pages without changing the story, they need to go. If those pages are full of information, find another way to weave that into the story so you can jump right into the heart of things. You don't have to set your story up—readers want the story right away.

10. Do the first few pages have a clear character voice that will pull readers in?

In my opinion, this is what sells books more than anything else. If I try a sample, and the voice pulls me in, I don't care if it starts with the weather or has the character alone, thinking. If I "meet" a character that I want to know better, I'll keep reading. Tall order, I know. How do you accomplish that in your novel?

One way is to write the novel to develop the main character's voice, and then revise to ensure the entire novel has that voice. It helps if you can get to know your character before you write the novel, and I include suggestions on that in the Character section.

I develop my novel ideas as a plot and character combination, helping me see and hear my characters before I start. (Some writers focus more on plot while others focus on character.) The characters should drive the story, so it's a good idea to nail them down before writing. To me, that doesn't mean a list of what they wear, look like, or eat. It's more about what's important to them, what embarrasses them, what they long for, what they would give anything to have… I also like to picture their mannerisms, favorite sayings, and way of speaking.

11. Does your first chapter match the tone and atmosphere of the rest of the book?

Sometimes authors put so much work into the opening chapter or scene that it's different from the story. I write my openings and move on, and then return to them after the novel is mostly done. After spending more time with the characters and story, I have a much better feel for the "world" of the novel. Then I can go back and ensure the beginning makes the right promises (based on the story) and sets up reader expectations for how the characters will act and talk.

12. Is the inciting incident big enough?

The inciting incident is not always the opening scene—in my novels it usually is, but there are different ways of doing things. Most authors start the story in an interesting and engaging way and move onto the inciting scene, the place where something happens that puts the character on a new course.

"Big" can refer to external or internal events, but something needs to happen to start the story. Something needs to change. Sometimes, it's a smaller event that feels big.

13. Is your beginning so overworked it's become awkward?

As an editor, I come across many manuscripts with awkward beginnings, and I can tell the author has reworked the heck out of it. They've gotten stressed and kept revising, trying to make it perfect. But the writing doesn't match the rest of the book. I see this in published books sometimes too.

Beginnings are hard. But they don't have to be. My advice is to forget about THE BEGINNING and just get into the story as quickly as possible. Jump right in and keep running—don't explain everything and all of the backstory.

Following are a few of my novel openings to show you how I jumped right into the story. These are in a separate section so you can also skip ahead to Plot & Structure.

Sample Openings

Stranger in my Bed

"Megan? Are you awake?"

It's not a familiar voice...or name. Who is Megan? I try unsuccessfully to move; I'm stone stiff, in piercing pain, and lying on something hard. In the background, I hear machine-like buzzing. An office? I wonder who he's talking to.

"Megan?" More urgent now. Someone takes my hand—a man. His skin is warm, bringing feeling back to mine. I turn my head toward the voice but I don't open my eyes. Who is he? Does he think *I'm* Megan? Everything is blank. I give it a minute, waiting for everything to come back. Like, oh, the party last night. Or, I'm in a hotel on vacation and that's why the bed feels strange.

Nothing comes back to me.

After another minute, still without anything surfacing, I squeeze his hand, hoping he'll say more.

"Doctor Harris!"

His hand pulls in mine as he turns away. Doctor? A hospital? That at least explains the jackhammer in my head.

"Megan, it's me, Eli. Can you open your eyes? Can you squeeze my hand again?"

The building pressure in my head is trying to blast my skull in a million directions. I want to reach up but it's hard to move anything or talk.

"Don't push her," a different voice says—the doctor he called for? This voice is rougher, gravely. Older. "She might need some time before she wants to respond."

"But—"

"But let's not rush this." A warning in the doctor's voice.

There seems to be more to that conversation, something else I should understand. In fact, there should be some bigger picture coming into focus here, making sense of all this. I force everything I have through my arm to squeeze his hand and hang on for dear life. The pressure in my head surges. I get my other hand to move toward my face.

"She's in pain. Can't you fix that?"

Everything fades away.

***

A Cowboy for Christmas

If her name meant anything to the tall cowboy who leaned against the porch rail, he didn't react. Instead, he appraised her with sky blue eyes while the afternoon light slanted against him. She'd pulled up to the house and introduced herself, and now waited for his name or a hello.

"The name ain't ringing a bell," he said quietly, then looked her up and down. "And believe me, I'd remember your face."

Would you now? It sounded like a compliment, but he didn't smile with it. Missy wasn't sure what to make of him.

His voice carried like a gentle breeze. The man, however, looked rough as the landscape around them. Hard stance, set jaw, arms folded. His long, lean body might be perfect for pressing against a woman, but his eyes were distrusting.

The sign clearly said Ocean View Stables, so she knew she had the right place.

"Melissa Nelson," she repeated. This was awkward. "Ben may have called me Missy." Come on, nothing? She rubbed her arms through her jacket, chilled from the cool Oregon weather and this overly warm welcome. "I'm Ben's sister. Aren't you Mr. Hatcher?"

"Nope." He tilted his head and stared some more, like he'd never seen a woman before. The daylight darkened. Raindrops plopped on her while she waited for some kind of answer. Any kind of answer would be nice. "Ben's lawyer called you," he added, "And you came right over. I see."

He wore a tan Stetson on his head, a rich blue shirt with sleeves rolled up, snug Wranglers, and boots. He'd make a great bedroom poster, something to ogle on lonely nights, but his too sexy look only distracted her.

Did she really lose her train of thought while checking him out? "I flew in from Nevada . . . He asked me to come." She almost added that Mr. Hatcher was supposed to meet her here. Wouldn't this guy know that?

"Come on in, then." Without introducing himself, he turned to the front door and led the way in. Inside, she fought off a shiver. It wasn't the cold this time, but a reaction to his nearness. His eyes were so intent on her, she could scarcely breathe.

Scents of leather and pine met her inside his home—a man's home for sure. "How did you know Ben?" she asked.

He opened a closet door and gestured to her coat. She wanted an answer, but decided to shrug out of her coat, since it was thin and wet anyway.

With his brows creased at her, he took it. "We went in fifty-fifty on this place."

Oh, no. She hadn't considered there would be other investors. That explained why he was here. "So you live here?"

"Yup."

***

Note: Of course, you don't always have to start right in the inciting incident, or with an argument or confrontation. This final example is from my novel *Point Hope* and shows a man dealing with a lot of emotional pain.

Point Hope

Trey held an aged picture in one hand, rubbing a thumb over it. It showed two young boys with dark hair sitting on the front steps together, a yellow lab puppy on their laps—the front half on Ricky's lap and the back half spilling onto Trey's cut-off jeans.

Trey had wanted the chocolate lab, but Ricky had begged and pleaded for the yellow one. It was a girl to boot, and Trey had wanted a boy dog. A boy like them. But his younger brother had fallen in love with that yellow lab, with her imploring brown puppy eyes, silky soft fur, and tiny pink tongue that licked them both

Even at that age, Ricky was a people person and knew how to be persuasive. It took just a flash of his little-boy smile, a tilt of his head, and his, "Aw, come on, Trey." So Trey had given in and let Ricky pick their new puppy, denying—of course—that Ricky had pushed him into it. There had been something special about the way Ricky had looked at that tiny dog and the gentle way he'd held her.

They'd named her together: Helen of Troy. It was a strong name, they thought, judging from a movie they'd just watched.

Helen had been gone a long time—she'd hailed back in the days of paper airplanes, secret forts, catching snakes, and baseball in the backyard.

Now Ricky was gone too.

A noise startled Trey, and he slipped the small photo back into his shirt pocket. He looked up as Rosette walked into their home office, noticing it took her a few steps to see him silently sitting in the brown leather chair in the corner. They'd been sharing the office, one person coming in when the other was out. The room had her mark all over it. She'd painted the walls a soft sea foam green. Her pictures and notes for their family history book were spread across their old oak desk. Her light purple sweater was slung over the armchair in the other corner—they'd picked out his-and-her chairs together a good six years ago. His sole decorating contribution was a large, framed photo of the Cape Arago Lighthouse, with the ocean and fiery sunset behind it, which he'd taken himself.

***

The reader soon learns that Trey and his wife Rosette are planning to divorce, but a death in the family has thrown a kink into everything. This opening is a childhood memory followed by the reality that his wife is a stranger to him now.

Plot & Structure

A good novel is like a good meal. Everything in a good meal compliments the rest, from the wine, hors d'oeuvres, to main course and dessert, creating an exquisite experience. The side dishes are perfect for the main course, and it's all presented well, letting you know you're in the hands of a master chef.

Likewise, all the elements of a good story strengthen the others: it's clear why this given character is in the story, and character and plot perfectly entwine to create escalating conflict, tension, and suspense. The writing is smooth and clear, and even insightful, letting you know you're in the hands of a talented author. (Or one that put in a lot of learning, work, and revising!)

That perfect balance begins with the premise and builds through the conflict, plot, characters, and writing. We've talked about openings. Now let's look at your plot and structure.

14. Is your plot logical?

Have you written out your plot points or looked over your outline to see if it makes sense? After each event and character action, would the reader be able to tell you why it happened? I call this the "Why Test." (Related is the "So What Test," a way to see if the event or action changes the story and means something to the reader.)

Do characters drive the plot with believable motivations? If anything feels farfetched, can you go through the earlier parts and write the set up to make it more believable? If something *doesn't* work, don't tack on a little explanation sentence or two afterwards. Readers will catch you. Instead, look at how you can add and strengthen details before that point.

15. Did you check your story order?

If something feels off, and you're not sure what, it might be the order of the story. A flashback might be stronger if it actually happens in the story, or a scene might be better in a different place. One newbie mistake is putting all the backstory in the beginning instead of weaving it throughout the story. Also look to see if you stick with one character for long periods of time; you can build more tension and suspense by switching back and forth more often.

If you have an outline, you can check the events and plot points there to ensure you have the most logical story flow. Beta readers might also notice if something is off with the timing or order.

16. Is your plot predictable?

This is one of the biggest issues cited by readers. Authors come back with, "Of course you've seen this plot before! There are millions of books! There are no original plots anymore!" So how do you make your story original?

Well, there actually are original stories releasing all the time. Maybe the plot structure at the very bottom is a common one, but the story itself is new and fresh. A romance is a romance, isn't it? A mystery follows a certain structure and route too. An "original" story does not mean that you re-write basic story structure. It means you add your own passion, experience, and skills. It means that the events (plot points) are surprising because they're not what the reader expects.

Sometimes I'm surprised not by what happens in a chapter, but how the author set it up and handled it. Maybe the event is predictable, but now your character can have a strange or unique reaction. (Just make it believable for your character.) A predictable event might even offer new and useful information or reveal that things weren't as they seemed. These are ways to add a twist—and that's what surprises the reader.

Look over your plot points and ask yourself: did you go with the first or second idea? Or did you dig deeper, and go with something that didn't come to mind right away? Maybe a scene feels predictable because it's too easy, and you could make it harder for your hero in that spot.

If you find some of the events in your novel feel obvious, you can still fix it. Why not leave the set up, but then have the character turn a different way and surprise us? You may need to weave in a few hints that your hero is planning something else so readers will believe it.

If you have a few events that are just too predictable and need rewritten, try using the other questions in this book to make the event bigger, more personal, more dangerous, or more surprising.

I often find that I can transform a scene with a few more lines and changes. It's like driving a car at seventy miles per hour: a small pull on the steering wheel results in a big change in direction. You can drastically change a scene with a few more character thoughts and emotions, insightful description of the setting that reveals character emotion, a line of dialogue that changes everything, or adding motivation behind actions.

17. Do you reveal information at the right time?

Is it too soon or too late? As late as possible is usually the strongest way, but make sure your characters don't use that information until they actually learn it. Sometimes, through rewriting, you might move a scene or detail, and then realize characters use something they shouldn't know about.

Did you reveal the information in the best way? Take a minute and picture what would happen if this information comes from a different character—would that make it more emotionally charged?

18. Does your story have three acts, the big plot points, and a resolution?

No, that isn't cliché. It's the format humans use to share stories most often, so readers recognize it and become more engaged.

The Three Acts are like a bridge that holds up your story: The inciting incident, building to the midpoint, and building to the climax.

This is a diagram from *Blockbuster Books, Broken Down* that illustrates my version of the novel structure:

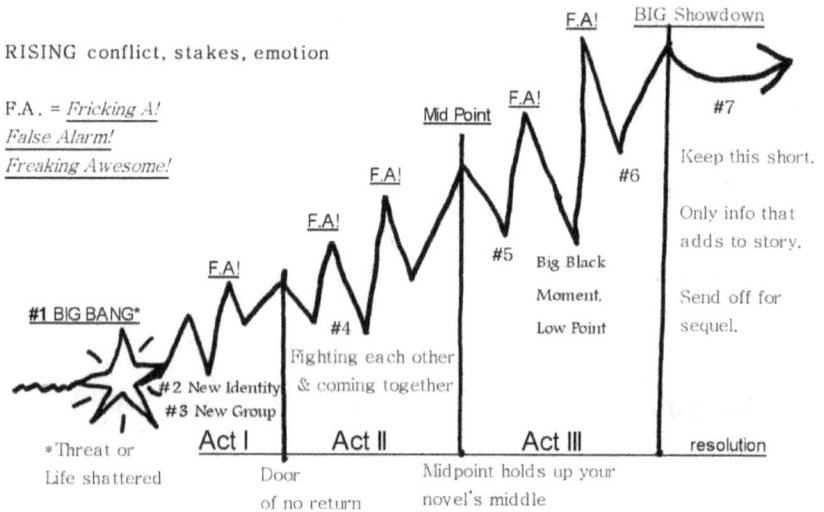

RISING conflict, stakes, emotion

F.A. = *Fricking A!*
False Alarm!
Freaking Awesome!

F.A!   BIG Showdown

F.A!
Mid Point

F.A!
#7
Keep this short.
Only info that
adds to story.
Send off for
sequel.

F.A!
#6
#5   Big Black
Moment,
Low Point

#1 BIG BANG*
#4
Fighting each other
#2 New Identity   & coming together
#3 New Group

Act I   Act II   Act III   resolution

*Threat or
Life shattered   Door
of no return   Midpoint holds up your
novel's middle

(Larger version after explanation.)

My diagram is different from the traditional model because I wanted to show how the story lifts the character to a new knowledge or way of life. The story is a long series of ups and downs with recognizable points along the way. This shows the big bang that opens your novel, the door of no return, the midpoint, and the climax, and those divide the story into three acts. There are also highs and lows, which I called F.A. points for frickin' A, false alarm, and freaking awesome.

Frickin' A: when all hell breaks loose, the enemy attacks, the lovers fight, a setback happens, something falls apart, or things go badly.

False Alarm: a lie revealed, a plan fails, hopes are dashed, a betrayal, an expectation isn't met, a trap, a trick, or a hoax.

Freaking Awesome: the high points when characters get to know each other, first kiss, first love scene, something actually works, a battle is won, a funny moment, a touching moment, someone is found, or knowledge is revealed.

Looking at your novel, do you have a variety of events based on these?

Let's look at the other points; I'll discuss the resolution in The Ending.

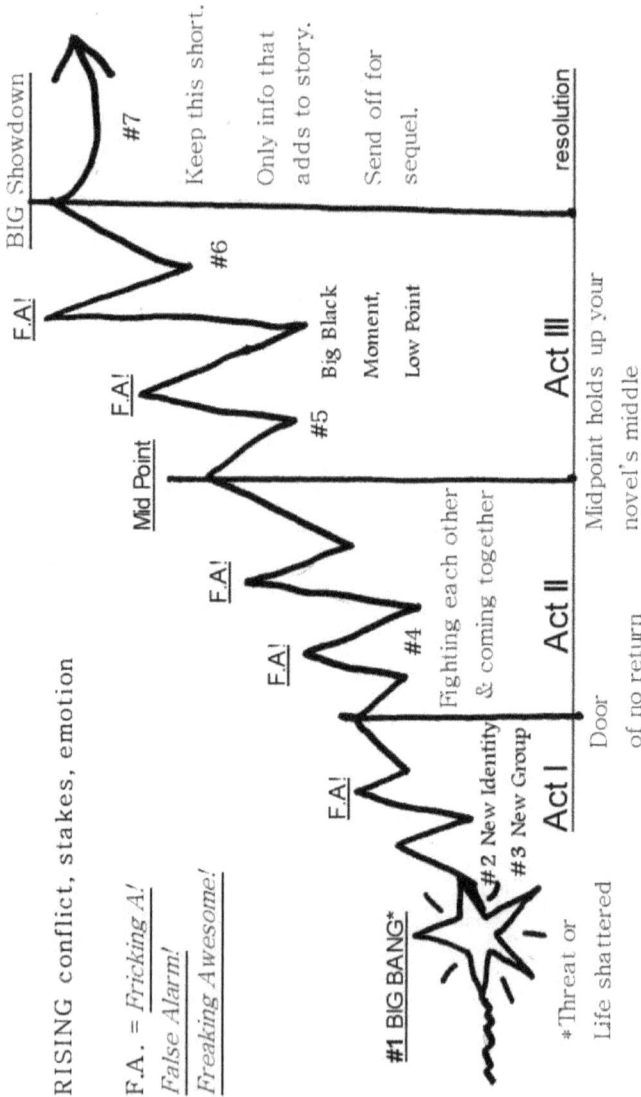

RISING conflict, stakes, emotion

F.A. = *Fricking A!*
False Alarm!
Freaking Awesome!

#1 BIG BANG*

*Threat or
Life shattered

Act I

#2 New Identity
#3 New Group

F.A!

Door
of no return

Act II

#4

Fighting each other
& coming together

F.A!

F.A!

Midpoint holds up your
novel's middle

Mid Point

F.A!

#5

Big Black
Moment,
Low Point

Act III

F.A!

#6

F.A!

BIG Showdown

#7

Keep this short.

Only info that
adds to story.

Send off for
sequel.

resolution

19. Does your story have a point of no return?

This is the transition from Act I to Act II, and it creates a door. The character makes a decision that changes things. They can no longer go back. This can be a "yes" or commitment, or leaving for a journey. It can also be a negative action: breaking a tie, burning a bridge, running away, or otherwise breaking loose from the old life in a way that forces them forward.

If you don't have anything like this, can you add a small point where your hero takes a step, says yes, or even has a bonding moment with another character that changes the course of the story? (And sends them toward the climax—you don't want a nonrelated event.)

In some of my romance novels, the door of no return happens very early on, even with the inciting incident. I like to get right into the heart of things quickly.

There are ways to customize the plot points, but having a story structure in place allows the reader to settle in because they recognize story.

20. Does your story have a midpoint?

This is a big turning point for your hero when she'll accept her fate, destiny, goal, or see what she needs to do. It's often very subtle but things click into place for the character and reader here. Your midpoint might be a line or paragraph, but it's pivotal to a story.

James Scott Bell has an entire book on the midpoint called *Writing Your Novel From the Middle*. (He has great stuff on structure in several books.)

22.   Are your plot points big enough, or can you make them bigger, deeper, more drastic, more meaningful, or more shocking?

Let's look at the big events in your novel, both inner and outer. Can you raise the stakes by making a threat more personal or adding a ticking clock? If someone betrays or hurts someone else, can you make that more painful, personal, or more of a betrayal? Can you make your big plot points even more damaging? Remember, the bigger the problems, the bigger the payoff and reward later on. This is all about pushing your hero over the edge. If you find yourself thinking, "I'm taking this too far..." you might be right on track.

23. Do you have clear conflict?

I've found that when an author works on a novel for a long time, they get muddled in the details and revising, and the central conflict may not be clear anymore. That doesn't mean you should give everything away in the beginning, but the reader should be able to understand the main force against the character.

Do you need to add information or details, or move something up closer to the beginning, so that the reader will see the threat?

24. Do you have any "easy fixes" in your novel, where it could be harder for the hero?

Solutions in fictional stories should not come from coincidence, a new character (benefactor) stepping in and saving the day, or chance.

This applies to new information as well. I've seen quite a few cases where a secondary character supplies needed information, but there isn't an explanation for how they obtained that information.

Plot and Character go hand in hand, so I'll cover characters next, and then Chapters & Pacing.

Characters

One crazy, counterintuitive thing I've learned about life and fiction is: people without obstacles don't go as far. Easy Street cruises through town but it doesn't go up the mountain.

Your characters need all kinds of problems to force them to grow. They should go into the novel with some issues too, maybe a past hurt, trust issues, anger, or a deep longing. All those will help you set up motivation for their goals. On that note…

25. Do your main characters have good motivation?

I qualify this with "good" motivation because some stories have weak or strange motivation that I don't buy. If you have to really stretch for the character's motivation, you might find tweaking their goal is a better way to go. Dig deep to discover why they really want what they want.

Sometimes character motivation is fairly clear and simple, and there is nothing wrong with that. A dad wants to save his daughter from her pimp because he loves her, and he wants her to have a better life. There could be deeper motivations there, but you don't always have to add more to make the motivation stronger. That might even dilute it.

Another good question to clarify motivation is, what will readers identify with?

26. Do your main characters have urgency?

Although some might argue my point, I believe urgency can be stronger than motivation. If someone you love is in mortal danger, you don't stop to consider your motivation for saving them. Why do your characters need to reach their goals SOON? That ticking clock cranks up the tension.

27. Do your main characters have *agency*?

Meaning, as much as possible, does your hero drive the story, meaning his/her actions make things happen? Agency is the ability to make decisions and change the story. If everything happens to your character and all they can do is react and survive, it'll make it harder to write a compelling story.

If your hero lacks agency, is there a way to tweak the plot so that it's the character's choice that caused the outcome?

The exception I see to this is young adult fiction where a teenager is thrust into a new world and needs to react. The redeeming quality in this case is how they change due to the events thrust upon them, and then they take action. To illustrate, think of Bella from *Twilight* or Katniss in the *Hunger Games.* They both eventually take action to change their lives; Katniss more so. But agency is usually better in fiction, and many successful young adult novels do have it. *Divergent* shows a young woman who steps out and takes action in the beginning of the story, even though it's hard. And *The Host* showed a strong willed human girl and a stubborn alien girl that share a body for a while.

In other genres, agency is very important. In mystery, the detective solves the crime. In thrillers, the person thrown into a life threatening scheme must figure things out before something kills them. In romance, the two people fight against the relationship but eventually fight *for* it. In women's fiction, the central character needs to make sense of her life in a new phase and then take positive actions. In adventure, the hero sets out to save the day.

Remember, a novel is a story of how a character changes, and then what they're strong enough to do.

28. Does your hero have a secret? Can you add one?

Or maybe another character keeps a secret from the hero. A secret doesn't work in every story, but when it does, it adds tension, depth, and mystery.

Did your hero tell a lie or mess up in some way? Can you add something big, or possibly a small lie that weighs on their conscience? Is it something fixable, or did this cause damage to another person? How did this change your character and what she'll do in the story?

29. Does your hero have an everyday flaw?

Maybe he's messy, loses things, or can't throw anything away. Maybe she's so shy that she seems stuck up. Maybe she's bossy at times. Maybe he's so protective of a family member that he stomps on others. There are many small flaws to choose from, and adding small and big flaws makes your character more believable. It gives them even more room to improve too, but small flaws don't always have to be fixed.

30. Does your hero(s) have an everyday fear?

Your hero might be driven by a big fear: not reaching his goal, losing a loved one, dying, not winning approval and love from someone, and the list goes on. But what about the smaller, everyday kinds of fears that we all have? These don't have to be rational. Since childhood, I've always been afraid of crocodiles in the rivers when I swim. I live in Oregon. We don't have crocodiles or alligators, but a crumpled maple leaf floating on the water sure looks like one to me.

These irrational fears can have a good reason, or even be partly rational. I guess I have a strange relationship with water. I love to swim in rivers, but I don't like going all the way under the surface, especially if the water isn't clear. I liked swimming under water as a kid, but it got complicated as I grew up. I spent my entire childhood in the same small town, and my class had around thirty people from kindergarten to graduation. A friend of mine drowned in high school. You can imagine it was a huge shock to our small community. Within a few years of that, I began wearing contacts, which make it harder to swim underwater. (They tend to fall out if you don't wear goggles.) Between the effects of those two things, I just stopped swimming underwater. I have a fairly good reason for it, but it's not completely rational, either. I've used this as a small element in two different novels because I can understand that fear of water and know it can become crippling if you let it. It's not the main conflict in any story I've written, but I've used it to add another layer.

In my novel *Costa Rica*, Annalisa is afraid of the water and going snorkeling. Drew and Annalisa are trying to fix their marriage while vacationing in Costa Rica, and he helps her with this fear when the group takes a boat out and snorkels for the day. It gives him the chance to protect, support, and help her again, while being patient and showing he loves her.

You might have a small fear or understand one that you can add to your story. Heck, if you understand one fear, it'll help you write about other fears. What about spiders and snakes? Heights? Public speaking? Are you afraid of clowns or know someone who is? If your hero has to run through a birthday party, carnival, or fair, why not make them afraid of clowns? It'll add another layer of interest and conflict.

Smaller, "everyday" fears make characters even more real and human. We can all identify with stress and little fears, and these can often enhance a novel. It doesn't take much work, either. You just need to add a new scene or even just a few lines in the first third of the novel. Your hero might see something on the street and shudder, thinking, *why can't clowns be outlawed? Instead they're running loose, scaring kids and giving people nightmares.* This makes your character opinionated too, another bonus. Adding those tidbits build your character and add dimension to your story.

31. Is your hero opinionated?

In real life, it drives us batty if someone is super opinionated. Have you ever spent the day with a two year old who wants everything *their* way? Or a grumpy old man who thinks he's an expert on attracting women and removing stains from the carpet, along with everything else in life? In fiction, however, it brings characters to life when they have a strong opinion: foods they hate, things they find gross, other people's habits that bug them, or how to do certain things. In *Something Borrowed* by Emily Giffin, Rachel shares a banana with a guy she's dating. He breaks off pieces for her, but he leaves the nasty end piece in the peel where it belongs. (Her words.) It's been about two years since I read the book, but I still remember that line. The character is "real" because of that.

32. Do your main characters have inner and external goals?

For Katniss, she wanted to stay alive in the Hunger Games (external) and wanted to protect her family (internal.)

To make this simpler, the external goal is the driving action part of the novel. The inner goal is often the real goal, in my mind. It's the why behind their external goal. There are lots of ways to look at it. If you're unsure about your story and character goals, ask yourself, "What is the hero trying to do?" and "Why?"

You most likely have the external goal. This question should clarify if you need to work on an inner goal or motivation, making your character more fully developed and *real*.

33. Do you have villain(s), and does the bad guy have redeeming qualities?

He adores his cat and spoils it rotten. She takes care of her elderly neighbor when she's not murdering other people. Bad guys can range from outright killers to nosy neighbors, and they should have a mix of good and bad qualities. A great example of this is the kid movie *Despicable Me*. Gru, the main character, is an evil villain by occupation but he turns out to be a nice guy with a soft heart.

If your story has a completely evil, repulsive person, can you add one good characteristic? Imagine a sick, twisted murderer who would give the devil nightmares…and then he recues homeless cats and finds them homes. It makes you stop and think about people. Stuff like that can even make you uncomfortable because you realize you might have a slice of evil in you if someone that bad has a slice of good in them. Life is like that too, and novels that reflect the convoluted side of life show human truth.

34. Does your villain have a good reason to be so evil?

Imagine how much stronger your novel will be if there is a reason your bad guy does the things he does. (Or she does.) Most of my novels don't have a villain exactly, but I did create one that I loved. His name was Alexander Pierce, and he grew up very poor, causing him to crave money and power. He became obsessed with a reporter named Cora, who also lived through tough times. In his mind, she should understand him. He had a good reason for all the horrible things he did: he did them for her. I actually felt bad for him because he couldn't have what he wanted, but that would have ruined the book!

If your readers can understand why your villain is doing bad things, it makes the story more complex and revealing. The villain is a hero in her life story, and even the villain thinks the book is about them.

35. Do you have a full cast of distinct characters?

If you have four or more important characters, do they feel distinct with their own motivations, goals, beliefs, speech, habits, responsibilities, and lives? Here's a way to test this: pick a character and see what would happen if you switched in your mother or father. Your favorite teacher. That guy from the office that talks your ears off. Janus from *Friends*. The idea is to take someone very distinct to you and picture them in your story. Do your characters have that effect? Are your characters so real that you can imagine running into them around town? And if you met them in real life, would they make an impression on you? Or are they like everyone else walking around Walmart?

Many authors like to make sheets for characters with goals, motivation, and conflict. You might also have sheets listing everything from their appearance, to history, to favorite foods. I like to look at their function within the novel—sometimes skimming through for that character's parts to see how they develop throughout the story. There are many ways to develop distinct characters, including:

- Clip a magazine picture of a model that looks like your character, and attach a sheet about their personality, fears, goals, habits, etc.
- Pick a famous person or a role they play in a film to use as your base character, and then build from there.
- Choose someone you've met or know that you could use as a base character. This gives you a starting point so you can picture their

mannerisms and speech, but then you fill in their fictional backstory, motivation, and goals. The end character might not be anything like the real person you started with, but this process really helps me see and know my characters.

I also recommend a book called *The Complete Writer's Guide to Heroes and Heroines: Sixteen Master Archetypes.* It includes a section that pairs all the types to show how a relationship might look. On the surface, you might think using an archetype would make a cliché character, but it gives you a fantastic base to build complex characters with lots of color. I especially love how the authors list characters from books and movies to illustrate each archetype.

If you only have two or three characters in your novel, can you add one or two more secondary people? In writing terms, we have "main" characters and "secondary" characters, but in many novels we have the main people, important secondary people, not-too-important people that have a plot purpose, and "walk ins." You don't have to give a character a lot of "screen time" to make them developed and colorful. Sometimes you can use a character type we all recognize, with an added twist.

36. Do all of your characters have distinct appearances?

I strive to mix up hair color, eye color, skin tones, builds, and clothing styles. This adds a layer of interest to the book, and can help readers keep characters apart. This is even more powerful if you can present distinct character voices in each different point of view.

37. Do all of your characters have distinct names?

Or do you have a Susan, Sally, Simone, etc? This is another one I catch when editing for others. The author created several characters with similar names: they either sound similar or start with the same letter. It can confuse readers who have to backtrack because their mind autocorrected the name to the wrong one.

Tip: if you change a character's name, you can use the Search and Replace function, but you should also do a final search for the old name in the final stages.

38. Do all of your characters want something?

That's where you get your conflict. Even in the *Hunger Games*, the characters wanted different things. Katniss wanted to take care of her family. Peeta wanted Katniss. Gale wanted Katniss and to overthrow the evil Capital. Haymitch wanted to drink and escape. Effie wanted her tributes to win the Hunger Games. There are even more characters in that trilogy that wanted other things.

Goals can actually be pretty simple and clear, and still be very gripping. Goals can also change throughout the book. In fact, the hero's goal might change at the midpoint: they go from fighting against their fate, destiny, or secret desire, to fighting for it.

It can get interesting when your characters all want something, and then they need something from the other characters. Sticking to the *Hunger Games*, Haymitch wanted to drink and escape, but Katniss and Peeta needed him to train them so that one of them might have some chance of surviving the games.

In my story *Stranger in my Bed*, Eli says he wants to help Megan and keep her safe, but she needs the truth from him.

You might be able to add this into your story, if it's not there already, by making one character want or need something from another character. This can be a small element in the story, but it creates more conflict.

39. Did you go overboard on the character profile, creating all kinds of unrelated details that you threw into the story?

It's important to get to know your character, but when you make up all their details, think about your story. Writing instructors talk about making a detailed dossier that lists everything from family history to clothing style, but be careful about creating your character away from the plot. Why not create the character's traits and history to play into the plot?

If you throw in a really weird detail about your character, readers will look for the reason. They'll wait for it to come up, expecting it to come into play at some point.

40. Do all of your characters have strong feelings about each other?

Working on this element truly adds another layer to your story. In life, we meet people and classify them right away. It's not often that we know a person but don't have any opinions or feelings about them. But we see that in stories all the time.

Sometimes I read or edit a novel and have a hard time telling the characters apart. This arises when the characters aren't distinct, but it's also caused by a lack of feeling toward each other. If your hero really dislikes another character, that will color the hero's description and interaction with that character.

Take a closer look at your work: make a list of all of your characters and then describe how your hero feels about them. If your hero doesn't feel anything that shows in your story right now, do you need to make that character more colorful? And by colorful, I mean annoying, more pushy, more opinionated, more deceitful, more secretive, more talkative, more silent, more helpful, more sweet, more of a pushover, more *something*?

Look at the relationship between all of your main characters. It might help to make a chart. Then think about how they interact and secretly feel about each other. You can have a lot of fun in this area, and it really deepens your story.

Just as an example of possible situations, imagine that your very best friend has another friend that you don't like. The three of you might do things together on a regular basis. So what do you do? Pretend to really like that third person? Talk to your best friend about it? Avoid the other person or decline to do things as a group? Things like this happen in groups all the time, such as when someone gets a new boyfriend/girlfriend and it changes the group dynamic.

Your "good guy" characters can all be a strong group but still have times when they get annoyed at each other or see each other's shortcomings. Which leads into our next question...

41. Do your characters have good and bad qualities?

People are complex beings. We need to take care of ourselves and survive, but we also have a driving need to take care of others, especially our family and friends. All people have good and bad qualities, and those can change around different people or in different situations. Many famous characters are full of bigger than life qualities that might be quite annoying in real life. Can you list good and bad qualities for your characters? More importantly, can you show their good and bad qualities in the story?

42. Do your main characters have conflicting beliefs or wants?

Sometimes we believe a certain way until life comes in and complicates things. Try this on: a woman is 100% prolife and against abortion…and then her twelve year old daughter gets pregnant. How on earth can she reconcile her beliefs with helping her daughter? What should she do? That's a scary situation to even think about.

In fiction, you don't have to make a stand for either side of your character's beliefs. You might. Or you might just want to have a complicated situation for your character, and a chance to show how messy life is. "Conflicting beliefs" can be smaller issues too. Let's say your hero believes in always telling the truth. That's an easy one to test. Or maybe your hero feels bad about pursuing his goal because it means letting others help him, or taking from others, or leaving people behind that he cares about.

As authors, we get focused on our hero's motivation and goals: there is one big prize that will save the day. It's nice that fictional characters can focus on something bigger than paying the bills and cleaning the house, right? But what if that goal is complicated? If your hero wins, someone else might lose that same thing. Or, winning might mean crossing some personal lines or breaking a promise.

What does your hero want? Can you add something to your story that makes achieving that goal both a win and a loss? For example, what if your secondary character also wanted that prize for herself? Or, let's say your hero wants to win a boating race…but then his father can't win.

With a finished draft, you probably don't want to rewrite the story, but you can add in some doubt or other thoughts to complicate the issue. However, if rewriting your story would take it from so-so to amazing by adding in a big element, go for it!

43. Do characters change in a big way by the end?

Does your hero know something new or understand life in a different way? Can your hero do something they could have never faced or tried before the story opened? That is the heart of story: how the hero changes. Like life, this change can be small or subtle but still profound. The "big" usually means an inner change.

- If you feel your hero doesn't change, ask yourself:
- Does the hero finally accept that he (she) can be happy? (You can add this in with a few thoughtful lines toward the end.)
- Does your hero realize it's okay? Life is good?
- Can your hero come to grips with what they gave up?

You can also look at your conflict—did your hero fight hard enough and give up enough to reach the goal? Maybe your hero lacks change because you need to up the stakes.

Strong characters create conflict and make the story. If you pick one thing to focus on, choose the people populating your books. That will help the other pieces fall into place. Of course we'll look at all the elements of a novel in this book, so on to Chapters & Pacing.

Chapters & Pacing

Pacing is a big part of a successful novel, and some might not realize the chapters help set the pace, along with paragraph length, scene length, dialogue, and writing style.

44. Are your chapters three scenes or less?

I like to have either three scenes per chapter, or one long, complex scene. The other option is to have one short, but very pivotal, scene. Many thriller writers use shorter chapters, sometimes sticking to one scene per chapter around 1500 words. Women's fiction usually has longer chapters. The real point is to use chapters to move the story.

45. Do you have clear scenes with changes in scenery, location, weather, and characters?

A story really moves when you change characters and locations for different scenes. Avoid sticking with a character for a full day unless the entire time is interesting with events, new information, or another reason to exist in the story.

46. Have you looked at your chapter openings and endings?

I love a book with good chapter endings, especially those little one-liners that throw in a new meaning, new question, new doubt, or somehow twist things.

47. Do you have any large chunks of back story?

Cut them! It kills story momentum. Often, it doesn't matter to the story. It matters to you so you can write your characters and plot, but readers only care about details that change the story.

48. Do you have any info dumps?

I've actually edited novels with pages and pages of family history. New writers are told to sketch out their characters with a full life of information, and then they might feel the need to include all of that together. Instead sprinkle it throughout the novel in thoughts, conversations, and possibly a flashback if it reveals something important.

Some novels require technical explanations. It can be tricky to incorporate information, resulting in "dear reader" dialogue. You can get away with that if your hero doesn't know the information and someone explains it. Readers do love to learn new things, as long as you sprinkle in your facts, or have someone teach the hero.

49. Is your manuscript a big chunk of thick text?

Or do you break things up and provide white space? When I edit, I find some writers tend to forget about paragraphs. These days, readers like more white space, meaning more paragraphs and dialogue.

Look through your book file. If it's solid words all the way across the screen, all the way down the page, readers are going to get bogged down. This often means you're summarizing instead of showing. Try adding more dialogue and action.

50. Is most of the story very short paragraphs and dialogue?

You can err on both sides: either too much thick text or very choppy, short paragraphs all through the story. Action and dialogue should normally have shorter paragraphs, and that should be balanced with meatier text throughout. Action, adventure, mystery, and thrillers have more of the shorter paragraph style, but you might also have a complex mystery with longer, more thoughtful sections.

Reading is a great way to get a feel for pacing in a story. Several times in this book, I recommend looking at your favorite novels. I love to read on Kindle, but you can learn even more when you have a print copy of a book. That way you can skim through for scene openings, plot points, chapter length, and more easily look at the balance of dialogue and action to thicker text. That will help you see pacing in action. It's just easier to flip around a print book. I've actually photocopied pages from published books and then marked them up to study the author's sentence structure and flow. (You can do that in the book too, if you don't mind marking up your copy.) If you have published books, you can do this with a copy of your own book. Flip through to look at the white space, if you vary your pacing as shown by dialogue and thicker text, and then sentence structure.

Of course, writing more books will also help you develop your pacing, style, and voice. It's exciting that we can always improve our craft.

Scenes

Scenes are the building blocks of the novel; each is another step in the journey of your story. With each new well written scene, the reader commits a little more to your book. The flipside is also true: a boring or confusing scene pushes the reader a step out of the story, giving them a moment to consider if they want to give you another chance.

Great scenes come in many forms: highly emotional, full of action, zingy dialogue, revealing, tense, satisfying, and even more. When writing a scene, I keep in mind the scene's main purpose and tone. What am I showing here, and how do I want the reader to feel about it?

51. Do you open each scene in the strongest way possible?

We give a lot of thought to our first line of the novel, but each scene is another opportunity to grab readers with a promise of story. Try to add conflict to that first line, even if it's very small conflict. Here's a subtle example:

Before: Jody arrived at the beach house around four, after everyone else.

After: Jody pulled up to the beach house, flustered, and noted that of course everyone else had arrived already.

If your scene is an argument, confrontation, or interaction with another character, can you hint at the conflict and tension in the first line? This can help set the scene, too.

No one answered her knock, so Jody stepped inside the house and into several loud conversations, catching squeaky voiced Heather midsentence: "...so embarrassed for her, and she has no idea!"

The first line of a scene can also jump with in with dialogue or in the middle of an action. It's really about pulling the reader in with emotion, conflict, or tension. Does your first line make readers go on to the second line?

For practice, take one of your favorite books and skim through, just reading the first line of every scene. That line won't always feel like a big explosion, but it usually makes you curious in some way. I just skimmed through *The Fault in Our Stars* to look at first lines—most aren't that earth shattering but are filled with Hazel's voice and personality. If you can do that in writing, you can do whatever you want to and readers will follow.

Next go through your manuscript and check out your scene openers.

52. Are your scenes anchored to a time and place?

I'm a "bare bones" writer, and I can accidentally write the main conflict of the scene and forget to fill out where it happens. When I go back through my first draft, I make sure to add a place for each scene, which can include:
- The actual location (in the house, car, beach, etc)
- Time of day
- Atmosphere and tone (through details)
- Weather if applicable
- Lighting
- Smells
- Feel of the air—too warm, caressing skin, burning cold, etc

Sometimes I like to add these details after writing the action and conflict so I can set the tone and atmosphere with the details.

53. Do you clue readers in at the beginning of the scene about who is there?

It yanks me out of the story if I'm reading along and a character suddenly speaks when I didn't know they were there. Don't wait until halfway through a scene to mention all the present characters.

54. Do you paint enough of the setting to allow the reader to be there?

This relates to the last question, and takes it one step further. Read your scene and think about the setting. Actually be there. Look around. Try to see this story place and what is has to offer that will reveal new things. In Strong Writing, I'll talk more about concrete and unique details.

55. Did you fully develop each scene by exploring character emotions, reactions, motivation, and thoughts?

When you write the first draft, it's easy to be skimpy on the inner life of your character. You might not know them all the way at that point, or know how they would react in a certain situation. You're also trying to get the story down, so it's perfectly fine in my mind to go through several times to fill out all the details. I'll write everything that comes to me, then fill it out more, and then revise it.

Once you have a first draft, however, it's important to explore each scene and reflect on how your character is experiencing the event. Do you show their thoughts and feelings through their inner life, and then have their actions either back that up or cover their real feelings?

You might have encountered this in a novel: something happens and the character doesn't react. You're thinking, "Whoa!" But the character is just moving on with things. Weren't they surprised? Or did they know? Did it hurt? How does it change things? What will they do now?

You don't have to spell everything out in boring detail. Be creative instead! An event happens and your character is sad—how can you show that in a less obvious way? You can mix methods, using emotion, thought, and action or lack thereof to paint your character's inner life.

56. Did you fill out around scenes with "life" to give feeling of realness?

Not everyone will have a problem with this issue, but I have to check my scenes and story to ensure I didn't leave everything too bare or sparse. I use a "bare bones" approach because I don't like fluff. The problem is, I can err on the side of not enough fluff. Readers like to get lost in the character's life, and that includes quirky things, taking wrong streets, making wrong assumptions, and little things that don't seem to directly drive the plot forward. You should build character and your story world, though. I'm not recommending lots of long description or going off on tangents, but a novel needs to be a reflection of life.

57. Do you paint the scene through the character?

Your point of view character should notice details that mean something to them *in that moment*. Don't simply paint the scene as if it's a flat picture for interpretation. What would your point of view character notice given how they feel and what they're going through?

58. Did you stick to one point of view?

Writers love to laugh at head hopping when they see it in a book. For most of the time, you should stay in one character's head in a given scene, showing only their thoughts and perceptions. This is called close point of view. If you throw in a thought from another character, it can confuse the reader.

In times past, authors would be a narrative voice over the story and share thoughts from all the present characters, in an omniscient point of view. A few big time authors still do this, so it's not the SIN some people make it out to be, but it's not popular anymore, and it takes skill to pull it off effectively and seamlessly. Unless you have a very good reason, I recommend sticking to the popular close point of view, which makes for a more personal story.

59. Does each scene move the story forward?

Every scene should reveal new information about the plot or characters: a secret, motivation, a new alliance, new clues, new traits, or some revelation. Sometimes the new information is subtle, such as character development. When you look at each scene, does it change the story somehow?

This applies to flashbacks too! A flashback should move the story forward by providing information that you can't show in any other way.

60. Would it change the story if you cut the given scene?

If not, you need to up the stakes and make more happen in this scene. If cutting the scene doesn't change anything in the novel, that means the scene didn't:

- Deliver any new information
- Reveal new motivations, secrets, lies, etc.
- Reveal a clue or show something was wrong
- Up the conflict
- Up the stakes
- Pull characters closer together (or rip them apart)

61. Is each scene a battle?

It helps some writers work on conflict and tension throughout the novel to work on making each scene a small battle. This can happen in many ways:

- Two characters want the same thing--competition
- A character wants to stop the other from something
- A character is lying or trying to hide something
- A character is trying not to hurt the other
- A character wants the other character—is that feeling returned?
- A character is trying to influence the other

There are many more situations and ways to do this. In mediation courses, there is a practice where two people are given sheets telling them what they want and what the other person wants in a scenario. The trick here is the two sheets don't match up. Each person thinks something that's wrong about the other person, thus creating confusion and tension. That makes it harder for them to work out the issue, unless they stop and clearly communicate, usually by asking questions. This exercise also demonstrates that people often go into a situation with the wrong idea about the other person and what the other person wants.

Now imagine doing this with your characters. People read other people wrong all the time. You can use that in your novel.

When you go through and look at your scenes, see if you can use confusion to add another layer of tension. Or, have both of the characters after something and being coy about it. The best tension is under the surface, but it's a battle nonetheless.

The great part about this is you can revise your scenes by adding thoughts, dialogue lines, and actions to add tension without always rewriting the scene. In fact, try leaving the existing material but adding in thoughts and actions that go against what seems to be happening.

62. Does something happen (inner or outer) in every scene?

It's very satisfying to read a scene where something external happens that illustrates what the hero is feeling. Readers tend to get bored if a scene is simply external or internal conflict without the other—we like to see what the character is going through and feel their emotions.

Using both inner and outer events will help you eliminate those "just thinking" or "all action" scenes. Of course, you'll want to lean toward inner or outer in most scenes, but you should have both. An action scene is more powerful when we get a little bit of the character's emotions and thoughts. And an emotional or thinking scene is better with some action and setting so we can see the character's world.

Scenes are like mini stories in your novel, and you can work on each like you would on a short story. Yes, they connect your novel, but a great scene accomplishes a lot. Try grabbing a novel and opening it randomly, then find the start of a scene to read. Reading scenes out of order like this can help you get a sense of what should happen in a scene and how to use different types.

Dialogue

Dialogue is a fun and different kind of writing. You can have your character say one thing while thinking something else entirely, and the reader gets to be in on it. You can also have your characters battling it out, using polite words with rude undertones. That's one example of where body language, tone, expression, word choice, and stressed words all come into play. Most communication is nonverbal, and writing "dialogue" should include all of the other elements too. In a novel, dialogue can even be a shortcut to show information if handled correctly. There are many great uses for when your characters speak.

63. Do you have natural dialogue?

And how do you tell? The best way is to write A LOT, and read what you write out loud.

It's beneficial to listen to how people speak, but make sure to write in that style without all the "um, oh, uhhh, and so on, and so forth…" You get the idea. In real speech, we stutter, start over, repeat ourselves, and say all kinds of little fragments that don't really make sense. Fictional dialogue should simulate life, but not too closely.

Natural dialogue:

- Uses contractions and fragments
- Uses that character's voice
- Doesn't always use proper grammar
- Doesn't always give an answer
- Doesn't strain to show dialect

- Is directed at the other character or thinking out loud, not directed at the reader to pass on information
- Uses other characters' names rarely (Not: John, I'm going to store. Do you want to go, John?)
- Shows emotion so you don't have to spell it out after the quote

Dialogue can speed up the pace of any passage and give it a "real time" feeling. It shows how two characters relate to each other. It's really a very fun and flexible writing tool, and I hope you can have fun with it!

64. Did you skip "Hello, how are you?" dialogue?

If you think about your favorite TV shows, you might notice scenes start after the characters are already talking. Or, they'll be walking down a hallway in a hurry, so there isn't time for small talk.

65. Did you avoid Dear Reader dialogue?

This is where the characters tell each other something for the reader's benefit. It's usually obvious and annoying. It's better to just fill the reader in using the character's thoughts, if you can't find a better way.

66. Do you vary dialogue exchanges so you have rat-a-tat-tat and longer, deeper conversations?

There are so many different kinds of conversations: information exchanges, a dance of lies, an argument, pillow talk, meaningful hellos and goodbyes, dry conversation that hides emotions, emotional conversations, and even quiet confrontations. If you glance through your manuscript, you can often tell what kind of conversation is happening by the way it looks on the page. Some conversations are all dialogue in short lines. These can be fun to read, especially with zingers, retorts, answering questions with questions, or just funny dialogue. These can also be angry exchanges, or two people on the run trying to pass information.

Your manuscript should have different kinds of conversations to set different paces, keep things interesting, and provide that life-like feeling.

67. Did you use body language, actions, and silence in dialogue?

I've noticed some newer writers will alternate between exposition and then dialogue that's all dialogue with "said" tags. So much more can be communicated with body language, noises, gestures, and silence. You can also use actions to show who spoke, and break away from using "said" all the time. (You don't want to replace said with fancy versions—use those like spices, just a dash here and there.)

68. Did you run a dialogue check for your main characters?

Each character should have their own voice and way of talking. Some characters have favorite sayings or even clichés. In my novel *All In My Head*, Marcus is a voice inside Avery's head. I used a special font for his lines instead of quotes, which made it easy to skim through the novel and pick out his lines. I was able to read his lines separately to ensure his voice was consistent, strong and clear. It's a little harder in a typical manuscript to read through for just one character. One way is to print out your novel and read it, highlighting the main character's lines in different colors. The point is to develop each voice to sound unique.

69. Do you avoid fancy ways to say, "he said"?

It's okay to use "he said," and "she said," because readers skim right over it. Using big, fancy, or strange words can throw the readers out of the story. Using "said" tells them who is speaking. Of course, you can use an action beat after the quote, which shows who spoke and what they're doing. For example:

Before: "I don't like it," he said, making a face.
Try: "I don't like it." He pushed the plate away and made a face.

Before: "WHY DID YOU DO IT?" he hollered.
Try: "Why? Why did you do it?" His fact twisted as his eyes filled with tears.

Before: "I'm so excited!" she exclaimed.
Try: "I'm so excited!" She rose up on her toes, bouncing, with her hands clasped in front of her chest.

A longer example:
"I can't take it anymore." Jenny wrapped her arms around her middle and turned away. "Knowing what he did to our brother is eating away at me. I can hardly eat. I feel sick all the time."
Kelly reached a hand out toward Jenny's back but dropped it.
"I know," she said, her voice barely audible over the breeze. "I try to pretend that happened in another life. I don't think about it here in this life."

*This has one "said" in it, but we can easily tell who is talking and see what they're doing.

70. Do you know when to use an alternate to "said"?

If you stick to using "said" and action beats, it will be more powerful when you use another term. For instance:

"I'm going to kill you now," he murmured, his voice as smooth as silk.

"I know you slept with Jimmy last weekend," he whispered. The noise around us stole his voice away so I had to lean in, questioning what I'd heard.

71. Do you have any spots where a character can outright lie—because the reader knows better?

This is a fun way to use dialogue. Let's say we readers know something, and in a scene a character lies about it. You don't have to say that it's a lie. Maybe hint by showing the character looking away, or feeling awkward or bad, or glancing at the other character to see if they noticed. There are lots of places in novels where a character has to lie or could lie. It's not an admirable characteristic, but it's something we've all had to do at one time or another. Maybe your hero needs to lie to save a life or to save someone from a deep hurt.

On the flip side, maybe you can have someone lie to your hero, and the hero knows it's a lie. The conversation doesn't reflect it, but we can see the hero's thoughts.

72. Do you understand proper punctuation for dialogue?

By this point in the game, you probably know how to punctuate. However, I see manuscripts with improper grammar, especially around quotes. Beta readers, editors, and proofreaders will catch these, but it's always good to know how to write properly. Here are a few examples:

Wrong: "I don't want to go." He said.
(Needs a comma, not a period.)

Correct: "I don't want to go," he said.
"I don't want to go!" he said.
He said, "I don't want to go!"
"Why don't you want to go?" he asked.

Now if you have a quote and then an action, you use a period:
"I don't want to go!" He spun around, slapped his book on the table, and stormed out of the room.

Here's an example of how to have a character quote someone else, using single quotes inside of the dialogue quote:
"She told me, 'I hate it here!' and ran out the door," Shirley said, shaking her head. "I can't believe she's treating me like this."

In most cases, you begin a new paragraph when a new person speaks. This is different in the rare case that your narrative voice is telling a story where several people speak. Then you can include all of these in one paragraph, but it's not wrong to use new paragraphs in that case, either.

Reading A LOT is one of the best ways to naturally learn good grammar. A few times I've been at a workshop or conference and heard an editor ask someone, "You haven't been reading much lately, have you? I could tell from your writing." I've always been curious about that. Could the editor tell due to poor grammar or awkward writing? Or I suppose it could have been both. Writers should be readers!

Sample Dialogue

This argument excerpt is Chapter 19 from *Stranger in my Bed*, written in thriller style with short chapters. I choose this because it mixes dialogue with Megan's thoughts and reactions, and uses action instead of "he said, she said" tags. (Contains strong language…and a slight spoiler for the novel.)

***

"Meg, you have to stop."

I startle so bad I send my notebook and pencil flying out onto the floor. Heat floods my face followed by a wave of icy cold. Eli stands in the bedroom doorway, hands on his hips, wearing gray sweats and a green T-shirt, wet from his run. His voice doesn't leave any room for argument but I try anyway.

"Stop what?"

"Stop making that list. Searching online. Prying into things." He takes four steps so he's standing over me.

He *has* been watching me. *Son of a bitch.*

I grab the notebook and slap it down on the bed to hide my writing, then cross my arms and glare up at him.

"This is why I didn't want to set up internet. You're going to get yourself hurt if you can't leave things alone."

"Give me one good fucking reason why, Eli. Is that even your name?"

He sits down, sighing deeply, like I'm a child in need of reprimand.

"Don't patronize me," I spit through gritted teeth. "Don't you *dare*. This is *my* life. I have every right to know why it's been turned upside down. And I know it has! I know this isn't right!" I push against his arm.

"Why am I here? If I know something that could hurt someone, why not just kill me?"

He jerks his head up. "What the hell do you mean by that?"

"Or is this all your doing?"

Eli jumps up, making me flinch a second time, and proceeds to methodically pace back and forth, sliding one hand over his hair one way and then the other. I watch, every cell in my body growing tighter and tenser until he swings to face me.

I hold my breath but he doesn't speak.

"Why can't I know?" My voice betrays me, making me sound like I'm begging. A new thought: what if there's a reason I'm alive? What if he needs me for something? "Eli?"

"We're in witness protection, Meg, to keep you alive."

***

I used movement to amp up the tension, but you can also cut dialogue down to just the spoken words to make it zing and move fast. To try that out, take an argument or snappy conversation and cut all the extra words; just leave the quotes and read it. You will probably add some of the surrounding text back in, but this exercise gets you to put more emotion into the actual spoken words.

Setting and Description

"Setting" can include your story world, the time period, any elements that are different from reality, and the way your character feels about his surroundings. This last item can add an entire new layer to a novel, and I don't see many authors use it. I set my novels in Oregon because I love living here, and my characters love it too, for the most part. It plays a bigger part in some stories than others, but my love of the area always helps me with description.

Setting and description are like icing: a little goes a long way. Sometimes you'll want to set a scene, but more often you can use a few concrete, unique details and let readers fill in the rest. In fact, if you go on too long describing a place or person, readers skim.

73. How does your character feel about the setting?

Does the hero love where he lives? Hate it? Does she see it as a stepping stone for the next adventure in life? Is it a hometown the hero wants to leave? How do you show your hero's feelings about where they are, or do you? If not, can you incorporate a few telling thoughts or lines of dialogue? It's better to sprinkle this aspect into the story instead of expounding on it at length.

74. Is your description filtered through your point of view character?

This is related to the last question, but different because this one looks at how your point of view character describes her surroundings. It throws me out of a story when description suddenly sounds like it's coming from the author. Here's a paragraph I made up to illustrate this:

Bobby shut the front door quietly and listened for any noise in the house before heading to the bedroom, where he promptly tossed the drawers. No cash there. *Tightwads.* In the closest, he felt all the pockets and found a fancy silver cigarette lighter. Nice. Might be worth a little, or he could keep it to look cool. He stuffed all the jewelry he could find into his pockets, then hurried to the bed and felt between the mattress and box spring. A picture up on the wall caught his eye, stopping him momentarily. It showed three generations: grandparents, parents, and kids, all dressed in their Sunday best and smiling broadly for the camera. Behind them, rhododendrons celebrated in a chorus of bright pink blossoms. The sky above them glowed in pretty baby blue, completing the perfect scene and pulling on his heart. If only he could have a family like that.

Now, this isn't the worst paragraph, but did you notice when I stepped in and described the flowers and sky in the picture? "Bobby" wouldn't have noticed those details in that way. You could cut those lines or change them to fit him better: "They stood in front of a bush full of flowers like they had nice property."

I find sections like this when the author did a terrific job of staying in character, but later added more description. Or maybe they just didn't think of filtering the description and details through their point of view character.

To fix this, pick a scene and step into your point of view character's head. What would this specific person notice about the surroundings? If they're stressed or scared, would they notice different details? Is this character a detail person, like a detective, journalist, or writer? Or is this character more emotional, so they would notice something pretty or a personal touch? Your character's mood will affect what they notice too.

75.   Does your setting complement the story's tone, or provide contrast?

The weather is a useful tool for setting the mood in your story if you stay away from clichés like a dark and stormy night as a backdrop to a fight. I like to contrast sunny weather to a stressful situation too—the character might notice how peaceful his surroundings are while his mind is spinning.

You have much more than the weather at your disposal. Pick a scene and step into it, and look around at what you can use to clue readers in to the mood.

76.   Is the story expansive enough, or can you add location changes or make the story cover more time?

A story should feel like a journey, and part of the technique behind that is covering enough time and space. You can give your novel a "big book" feel by moving to a new location several times and covering a longer period of time.

This question has been on my personal list for the last two years. One of my better selling novels, *Point Hope*, covers just a few weeks of time, and the story mostly happens in and around the family's home, with a few trips to other locations within their town. Most readers love that story, but some called it "shallow" in their reviews. It took me quite a while to pin down where that feeling came from. It's a deeply emotional story about a couple fixing their marriage and saving their family, but I think the short time period gave a "small book" impression to some readers. Looking back, I see that I could have added in a week or even a month by skipping forward in time or showing a few scenes within that time. *Point Hope* is women's fiction, and that kind of reader usually prefers longer books that span more time. I've also learned not to point out what day of the week it is, or that only a week has passed. I used to print out my manuscript and go through to mark each day. If you don't mark days in a story, it gives a sense of time passing, and you can describe a few days while the reader gets a sense of more time passing.

Do you read novels that span a decade or a lifetime? Look at how the author did it. New chapters will start years later, and they don't spend any time catching you up on what happened in the missing time. We just assume not much changed. It's easy to skip forward in time with a small introductory phrase:

- Autumn arrived with dark, stormy weather, and Alice liked the change.
- Tourists arrived with the warm weather, and life came back to the town's streets.
- An entire year had passed and Andrew only gave me a passing nod when he saw me again.

Some genres, like mysteries and thrillers, can get away with a story that lasts just a few days. (That doesn't mean you have to do that.) They have *a lot* that happens in every day, with multiple locations, characters, and escalating conflict and suspense. They might still skip forward in time.

77. Are you purposeful with your setting?

Do you use the setting to set the mood, or provide information and insights on your characters? Does the area change during the story? Maybe the character's view of the setting changes during the story. The setting can be a very useful tool in many stories, and not all authors think to use it. Hint: you don't have to describe the setting in long, detailed passages. Instead filter a few insights through your character's thoughts.

78. Could you move your setting to somewhere else to add another layer to the story?

This might sound like a crazy question, asking if you should move your setting in a finished draft. However, it could prove useful if you feel something is lacking and the story just isn't exciting. Think of *Water for Elephants,* set on a circus train. Imagine if the main character had never left his school, and the story happened there. The circus is a huge element of the story.

You might have an "anywhere" setting, and you could move the story to a place with some kind of interesting attraction or history that would add color to the story.

79. Are you using the setting to its full potential?

You may already have your story set someplace very interesting, but do you show that in the story? Have you explored the area for inspiration? What real history can you pull from your setting and put into your story?

If you're using a fictional town or setting, could you add interesting history or elements?

Used correctly, setting is a powerful tool that can reveal insights about your characters and story, and add color and interest. It should remain in the background, but an interesting setting is like a brilliant sunset behind your action.

The Ending

I've heard that beginnings sell that book while the ending sells the next. So, let's start with the most important question...

80. Is your ending emotionally satisfying?

To answer this, think about:
- How hard was it for your characters to get here? Did they pay a high price?
- Did your hero bring about the ending? You don't want a "reaction" ending.
- Is the ending emotional—the payoff matching the effort?
- Did the hero find what they needed?
- Did the hero get a new understanding, especially if they were seeking some kind of answer to life?
- Did the hero(s) change for the better in some way?
- Did the bad guys get what they deserved?
- Does the story and ending show the reader something new about life?

81. Did you answer all the big story questions?

This plays into the last question. The big questions in a novel, even if there are more books to come, should be answered. You can answer the questions raised throughout the novel *and* introduce new questions for the next book.

82. Did you wrap up the subplots?

If there isn't a sequel, you need to wrap up the smaller story questions as well. In my novel, *All In My Head*, I wrapped up the big storyline between Marcus and Avery, but left open several threads between Avery and her friends. I tried to give a sense that she was a stronger person now and would go fix those problems after the story closed. I didn't intend to write a sequel, but now readers are asking for one. They want to see those smaller story threads worked out. So if you don't plan to write another book, give some kind of answer for the smaller questions. Instead of completely fixing those issues, you can alternatively show a moment where the characters in the subplot come together, showing they're going to fix things. But it's very satisfying if all the loose threads are tied up at the end of a novel…just not too tightly.

83. Did you wrap things up too tightly?

I know, I can hear you: "What do you want from me? Wrap it up, but not too tightly?!" Yes, a good ending is a delicate balance. You should complete your story threads, but fiction can be a little messy and open ended like life. If everything works out perfectly, without any sacrifice or bending at the end, it feels too pat. We know when we accomplish something or finally arrive at a goal, it's not 100% peachy and perfect. Things usually work out a little differently than we expected, and we're okay with that. Sometimes, we had to bend in our thinking and change, let go of things, grow, and give up a few things that were dear to us. Your novel ending should reflect all of this. The hero wins the day, or the couple gets together, but it should come with some kind of price, even something as seemingly simple as a new understanding that comes with responsibility.

84. Does the story have a climax and then resolution?

You should have some kind of big showdown or pivotal scene where the conflict comes to a head and everything explodes. After that, the wrap up should be satisfying, but in my humble opinion, short. Give them what they need and get out of there, maybe leaving a little room for the reader to wonder about the character's life afterwards.

85. Did you simply end the story, having chance or a benefactor fix things?

A fairy godmother works great for Disney, but that kind of ending usually leaves readers let down. If you're really stuck about how to dig your characters back out, ask beta readers what they think.

Related to that, if you have a cliffhanger (for a sequel) do you still wrap up some story questions and give your hero a reason to continue on? If everything is lost and the hero wants to give up, it's not much of a cliff hanger. That's just a depressing ending.

Another thing that pops up in Amazon reviews is, "The book just ended, like the author got tired or had a deadline." Yup, readers catch us if we cut corners. They need that balance where the story is wrapped up and concluded, but not dragged out.

Study endings in your favorite novels. Look at the last few chapters to see how much resolution they provided after the climax. Do you remember skimming an ending in a certain novel? Take a look at those as well to see how they could have concluded the story sooner or better.

86. Did you tie in theme or link to life in the ending?

This gives readers a sense of an open ending that is satisfying.

This is harder in genre—in romance, readers really want a big, emotional, romantic ending. But any story can have a thoughtful line or paragraph, if you don't overdo it. Remember subtle additions can make big changes!

The theme in *Point Hope* is that love, marriage, and family are worth fighting for. This is woven into the story, and at the end the main character Trey gets up to speak at a funeral. (There are sad elements too.) I took my theme and let him talk about it. It's not a long talk, but I felt it was powerful for him to express what he'd learned from the past weeks. (That's also a case of where it's okay to tell instead of show, which I talk about more in the next section.)

In your novel, can your hero share a thought with another character? Or have a closing thought at the end? It might seem obvious to put your theme into words like that, but it can be emotional and fulfilling for readers. Think about how someone would really express that sentiment. They wouldn't say, "What I learned is…" It would be a thoughtful and reflective comment, or in some novels something sassy.

Like beginnings, novel endings can be hard. But remember you've had the entire novel to set up the ending. If you've written a strong novel, the ending will flow naturally from the characters and events. Does your ending make *you* emotional? Step into your reader shoes and reflect on your story and ending. Beta readers are a great resource too. Lastly, compare your ending to your beginning—did the character come through hell and change? Or did the story come full circle? Or does life feel different now? A novel's ending should feel like the end of a journey for the reader. If you've given them that experience, they'll be back for more stories.

Strong Writing

"Strong writing" can mean so many different things! I define it as expertise in the mechanics of communicating your story from you to the reader. This includes a clear voice in the text, proper grammar, vivid details, poetic language at times, and the ability to make the writing disappear so the reader can experience the story. It's okay if a reader pauses to appreciate the picture you're painting or the sentence you wrote, but too much of that will remind them they're reading.

87. Did you use concrete, unique details in description?

The more concrete and specific the detail, the more the reader can picture the story. I like to pick a few details that paint the broader picture.

A truck can become an old blue Chevy with chipped paint.

The rain can be a slow drizzle, matching how the character feels she's living a slow death in her desolate tiny town.

88. Did you use concrete, unique details for emotions?

Personal experiences are a goldmine for describing emotions in new ways. Imagine your character is extremely angry. Then remember a time when you were so mad you couldn't even form a sentence. You can take details from your experience to enrich the scene. The situation doesn't have to match. The emotion doesn't have to exactly match either. Your character might be so angry they murder someone. You didn't go that far, but you've felt anger.

I keep a list of emotional experiences. Each item is just a few words, but reading them can take me back to the middle of that experience and then I can explore how I felt and what I noticed.

Hint: I really like to read emotion shown through the character's thoughts and details they see instead of what's going on inside their body. Newer writers use speeding heart beats, swelling hearts, sweat, racing minds, etc to describe emotions. Those can be clear and useful, but they're used a lot too. If you think back to an emotional experience, you often think of details around you. Using both can make character emotions more comprehensive.

89. Did you use any unrealistic details that will throw readers out of the story?

I read a book this last year with a wreck fairly close to the beginning that involved a "five ton pickup truck." I'm a country girl living in Oregon, so that made me stop. A five ton truck is like a dump truck. It's huge. A pickup is small vehicle, on the other end of sizes for trucks. This is a case of a very small detail turning into a big deal, at least for this reader. It was still a great book, but that instance made me think about the details we use in writing.

When in doubt, double check. If you're not familiar with something, you can search online to check out pictures, its history, how to use it, where to buy it, when it was invented... The list goes on and on. I use Google several times a day to double check a fact or even how to use a word. I might write a sentence and then pause because I'm over thinking a certain word, so I'll "google" it to ensure I'm using or spelling it correctly. If you google a word, the definition and examples come up so you can check all of that with a glance.

90. Did you use all of the senses?

You don't have to use all of the senses in every scene, but they should be throughout the story. I like to break them down into more than just the five senses. This list helps me use concrete details:

- Colors
- Brightness, matte, shiny
- Tastes – sweet, sour, how it feels in the mouth
- Scents and smells—can you also feel it in your nose or taste it in the air?
- Temperature
- Dry, muggy, or crispy
- Windy, still, or soft air
- Sounds, including rhythm and patterns
- Texture or smoothness when touching something else
- How something feels as it touches my skin

91. Did you look at your paragraphs for flow?

I like to read scenes after I finish writing them, and often again the next day, to check the story and flow in each paragraph. This is something you can check again when you read through your first draft, and even again when you proofread the book. It's amazing how something will suddenly jump out at you on the fifth time through.

When you go through your novel looking at paragraph structure, you'll suddenly realize a sentence at the end should be up higher. You might have a descriptive sentence at the bottom of a paragraph, and the reader needs it at the beginning to picture the setting. Or your action could be out of order. Or you might mention a character at the end of a paragraph, and readers didn't know that person was there yet.

The first draft of this book had two sentences together that read:

"On the web, content trumps all. In fiction, it's all about the story."

These sentences are okay, but they presented an opportunity for parallel construction:

"On the web, content trumps all. In fiction, story is king."

It's a small change, but it improves the flow and makes the important part of both sentences read in a similar way.

92. Did you use passive voice?

An easy example: the book was given to her.

A fun way to check for this is to see if you can add a phrase like "by zombies" at the end. The book was given to her by zombies.

For the most part, passive voice kills momentum in fiction. Some writers accidentally use it when trying to vary sentence structure, or because it sounds literary to them. Readers usually don't like it as much.

There are a few times when you can use passive voice on purpose, especially in dialogue:

He looked down and shrugged before saying, "Mistakes were made."

Here are two examples that aren't exactly passive voice, but it's a useful way to tweak it and build conflict:

"Kelly, that's a pretty necklace."
"Thanks, it was a gift."
(Notice she didn't say who gave it to her… an ex boyfriend?)

"Wow, you're good at this," Melinda said as Jason rubbed her shoulders. "How did you get so good?"
"I was taught…"
(By whom? Seems like he wants to leave that out."

Related to passive voice is a sentence structure that employs –ing. I've gotten manuscripts with paragraphs full of these. For example:

Walking into the room, she looked around for her friend Amanda. Spotting Amanda, she waved and went to sit down with her. Because she had run all the way here, she was out of breath. Laughing, she tried to explain.

I see this sometimes in published work, but not always to this extent. It's a good idea to vary sentence structure, but once again you don't want to do anything that will throw readers out of reading. You can err on the other side too, especially in a paragraph full of small actions:

He opened the door and went inside. **He** could see the room had been tossed, so he pulled on rubber gloves. **He** started with the items on the floor closest to the door. **He** didn't find any clues there so he proceeded to the kitchen.

This paragraph uses filter words too, which is listed a few items down. You can switch this up by throwing in a thought, or starting a sentence differently: The picture was upside down, and he flipped it over to find the photograph was missing. Interesting.

93. Do you know when to show and when to tell?

Did I really write that? Are the gods of fiction going to come after me?

"Show, don't tell" normally applies to writing. No one likes to read summary or lazy writing. However, there is a time that telling can be powerful.

A character has an epiphany:
I'd been searching for the truth for years, but it was inside me all along; I just didn't believe it.

The line sums up everything the character felt at the end of a scene:

All that anger and hatred simmered together, congealing around my heart. It was wrong and selfish, but there it was.

A thoughtful first line:

Of course I didn't know it just then, but this little event would make me question my sanity and everything about my life. (From *All In My Head.*)

You can catch places where you *told* and should have *shown* by searching for the word "was."

It was a rainy night.

Or: Rain poured down so loud we couldn't hear the TV.

Also look for spots where you summarized conversation or events, usually given away by big chunks of thick text.

94. Do you use filter words?

This especially happens when writing in first person. Filter words put a layer between the reader and the story. Let me show you an example in third person.

With filter words:

She *felt* her head bounce off the ground, and then *heard* screams behind her as her friends ran to her. At first, she only *felt* dizzy, but a second later she *felt* a shattering pain overtake her, sending her down into darkness.

Without filter words:

Her head bounced off the ground. Screams shattered the air behind her as her friends ran to her. At first, she only felt dizzy, but a second later shattering pain overtook her, sending her down into darkness.

I kept one instance of "felt," and you could rewrite that bit into something stronger too.

Filter words slip into writing in first person because you, as the writer, are trying to filter everything through your character. That's even good writing advice. I caught myself doing this in my novel *Stranger in my Bed*. The character woke up from a coma and described all the sensations as each sense came back to her. I reworked it to take out all the filter words, and it read so much better and pulled me directly into the fictional room.

You can catch these by reading through your work and searching for certain words, such as:

- See, saw
- Notice
- Watch
- Hear, heard
- Look
- Felt, feel
- Wonder
- Realize
- Seem
- Decide
- To
- Turn (as in turning his head to look)

Using this, you can change, "he turned his head and noticed the tiny hummingbird," to "Something buzzed by his head. A tiny hummingbird paused in the air to look at him before flying off."

Writing well is a lifelong pursuit, and I'm sure I'll learn many more ways to make my prose shine. Remember, too, that story is key. Readers are buying a story, not a collection of sentences that would impress your college English professor. Use your words to paint your characters and events.

Final Checks

95. If your draft is complete, did you compare the novel to the outline for any loose ends?

Did you answer all the story questions in some way? (An open ended answer or solution is better than not addressing a point.) I like to ask my early readers (or beta readers) what questions came up for them during the story. Then I check if I answer those by the novel's end.

96. Did you check your story threads?

"Threads" can refer to a full subplot or a small aspect of the story that goes all the way through. When I'm working on this, I get a picture of brushing long hair. At first there are many tangles that stop the comb, but the more you pull the comb through, the smoother the hair becomes. Stories have many threads, and it can be easy to plant something and never deliver, or bring something up several times and never resolve it. This can be referred to as set up and pay off, when done correctly.

97. Did you check for point of view problems?

This includes switching between first and third person and head hopping. If you're in one character's head, you can't share a thought from another character.

98. Did you stay in the same tense for the entire novel, unless you purposely changed for different chapters/characters?

Typically you want to stay in the same tense unless you have a good reason. I've read novels where the prologue was in a different tense, or a certain character got chapters in a different tense. I'm not sure it added to the story to be honest, but I know authors like to play around with format and story.

Some newer writers will accidentally switch between past and present tense. They'll get caught up in a good scene and move from past to present. When I moved on to a new project in a different tense, I've caught myself falling back into routine.

How to catch this: Normally you'll see this when you're reading a passage or editing. If I catch any instances of this or another issue, I'll skim through the book for it, or find a way to search for the issue using the Search box. I've looked for accidental usage of the past tense by searching "ed."

99. When editing, did you use the lazy "add on" instead of making a change?

This is a personal pet peeve of mine, and I see it in quite a few novels, even ones that are doing well. I'll read a line that goes against what I know from the story set up so far or the scene set up, and then the next line throws in some information to fix it. Let's say a character suddenly has a useful item. I wonder, how did they get it? Didn't they just rush out of the burning house without anything? But the next line will say, "Tina had slipped back into the house to grab it at the last second."

Wait, what? Why not go back and add that detail where it belongs. Then it looks like good writing and set up instead of a slip up. I think these happen because the editor will make a note saying, "Wait, she rushed out of the house and didn't have anything." So the author adds a line right there to explain it. But it doesn't work for me.

A few other examples of this:

A character knows something they shouldn't, and then a line explains that so-and-so told them yesterday. If it's a critical plot point, you need to set it up.

A character knows how to do something that provides a solution. If it's something not too likely, it should be set up earlier in the novel. Readers recognize those set ups, too. They'll learn something about the character and think, "Okay, that'll come up again."

100. Do you have a list of your common mistakes, and did you search for those items? (And do you know proper grammar?)

We all have words that we overuse, misspell, misuse, or confuse, and it will benefit you to check these before sending your book to a proofreader. For one, you'll look better, but you should catch everything you can. Proofreaders miss things once in a while, so you can produce an even cleaner book by checking issues you know about. I keep a growing list of anything I know I do, so I can search my work for those words. (You can do a last check using Word's search function.)

My list includes things like:
- Woman/women
- Dinning for dining (the correct word for eating out is dining)
- They for the
- Out for our/ our for out

You can search online for commonly misused and misspelled words as well, and add them to your list of things to check. If you keep a list, add to it whenever you notice you did something, or an editor points it out. I might add something to the list even if I only did it once, just to check it a few times. There are times when I misuse a word I know too. My mind is picturing the story when I write, so sometimes my fingers do their own thing! English is one complicated language with words from all over the world and rules that don't always apply. Thank goodness for editors and proofreaders.

Here's a list of commonly misused words:
- Desert/dessert   (desert is a dry place)
- Their/there/they're
- Then/than
- Lie/lay
- Set, sit, sat
- Flare/flair
- Its/it's (its shows ownership)
- To/two/too
- Effect/affect (you affect something, and then see the effect)
- Your/you're
- Accept/except
- Allusion, illusion
- Elicit, illicit
- Principle, principal

We could build a much longer list, of course. If you search online for "commonly misused and misspelled words," you will find grammar websites and a Wikipedia page containing an exhaustive list of words along with examples and definitions. The point of your list is to know what you mix up or overuse, so you can check your writing before passing it on.

And for the second part of this question:

Do you understand grammar, and know your overused punctuation?

No one wants poor grammar or writing to scare off readers. I'll share a few insights here, but if you have trouble with grammar, pick up a few books and read online.

When line editing, I find myself moving comas on a frequent basis. People who have been writing for several years get the hang of it, but many people who don't write for a profession seem to either misuse commas or not use them at all. They're funny little things. I tell people to put a coma where you pause when speaking, but I've found that many people pause in odd places to color their speaking.

The most common coma mistake I see is putting the coma after the word "but."

Wrong: I went to the store but, I forgot my wallet.
Correct: I went to the store, but I forgot my wallet.

That comma goes after the first sentence of, "I went to the store." You put in your comma and joining word "but," and then add the next sentence, "I forgot my wallet."

You can find these by searching for, "but," in the Search box.

Now for the other part of that question: do you overuse a certain punctuation mark?

Some people love exclamations! They use them everywhere! Even when they don't need them!

Other people like to add question marks to statements like this one?

And some writers absolutely love to end everything in an ellipsis… Like every sentence… Because they imagine their character's thoughts trailing away…

A few writers like their semicolons; maybe they think it looks smart to use them a lot. I've seen writers use them as commas; so when they make a list, they say butter; eggs; salt; pepper; and bacon.

And lastly, while it's not exactly punctuation, we have Writers who use Random capitols in their Sentences. I haven't found a Rhyme or reason for this one Yet. Maybe they felt that word Needed emphasis?

I've caught myself with a few of these, overusing ellipses or having two semicolons on the same page. You don't want to use those too often in fiction. I should also say there are a few exceptions. If a character (like a teenager) makes a statement in dialogue but it sounds like a question, then it's okay (in my mind) to have a question mark.

101. Did you do a final read through after all the editing and proofreading was done?

When you work with a traditional publisher, they send you the final file for the last read through *after* it has been edited and proofread. You would think at that point that the manuscript would be clean, but things still pop out at me. I published *Point Hope* in 2013 and then sold republishing rights to Montlake Romance later in the same year. So the book went through my production process and then theirs. When I did the final read through for them, I still found a few things. There was a paragraph with five instances of the word "had." It was a very short flashback, so the word "had" was proper grammar, but it didn't read well. I had cued the reader in that it was a memory, so I went ahead and removed "had" to make it flow better. I also found a few words that weren't the right one: an instance where I talked about a "sandy" jetty when in fact jetties are rocky.

I do my final read through check by saving the file to PDF and enlarging it on my computer screen. That way it's easy to read, but I can't start editing, adding, or changing things, and I stick to a final check for any last typos, errors, or formatting issues.

I might alternatively send the file to my Kindle to read, and write down any typos I see. (You can send a Word file or PDF by using your

Kindle email address. It's listed in your Amazon account under Devices.) Some authors always do a final check on printed paper, and say they catch much more in this format than reading on a screen. If you're self publishing, after all of the other checks, you can order a printed proof copy and read through that.

Share Your Book!

I sincerely hope these questions helped you find many elements to improve in your work, and maybe you saw items you've got covered already too! That's always a good feeling.

I've encountered a few views out there on when to publish. One says you should toil away for years, revising until you can't see straight. I say, put in the learning, writing, practice, revision, proper production steps, and then share your novel.

On one hand it's true that the world doesn't need another novel, but on the other hand it *is not* true. The world does need more stories. Your book is different from every other book. People will always need new stories. In fact, stories set us apart from all the other creatures on this planet. We imagine and create; sharing stories is a crucial part of our existence.

Your novel might have 500 or 500,000 "right" readers that will get your writing style and love your story. If you submit to agents and publishers, it's possible that you might sell your manuscript, and it's also possible that none of them are your right reader. Don't give up. Your readers are out there. If you have passion for your book and have put in the time, make it happen. Publish that book one way or another. I'm all for Indie publishing, going with an agent, or submitting to publishers directly. It's your writing career. In the end, the publication method is simply an avenue to reach readers. That's why we write: we're creating stories for readers to read.

***

About the Author

Authorpreneur, Editor, Speaker

Kristen James is an outdoorsy girl who loves hiking, picking wild berries and mushrooms, and spending time with her family. Of course she loves reading and writing too! She discovered writing in the fourth grade when her class wrote short stories. Now she writes love stories with a twist of mystery and suspense set in the rugged and beautiful Pacific Northwest.

James is the author of four other nonfiction titles for authors and twenty-five works of fiction. Her books have ranked in the top 100 Bestsellers in Kindle US, UK and Canada, #1 in ten different categories, and #1 in Movers & Shakers and free rankings.

Connect and learn more at www.writerkristenjames.com

Feedback or comments on this book?
kristen@writerkristenjames.com

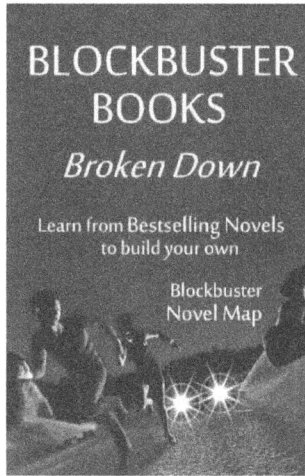

Blockbuster Books, Broken Down

Learn from mega bestselling novels to build your own breakout plot!

Why start from scratch and reinvent storytelling? Instead, use a 7 point plot outline developed from wildly successful novels.

"Blockbuster Books, Broken Down" is a workbook style guide that reveals the structure and elements in huge bestsellers of the last fifteen years, many of which became movies. By breaking down these books, we can see how successful authors are breaking out by satisfying readers' needs.

Part 1 deconstructs today's bestsellers and offers insights and keys to blockbusters and the Blockbuster Novel Map.

Part 2 guides you in creating a breakout idea and developing that into a solid plot with a novel map. Build from the ground up with 7 points to ensure your plot will connect with readers.

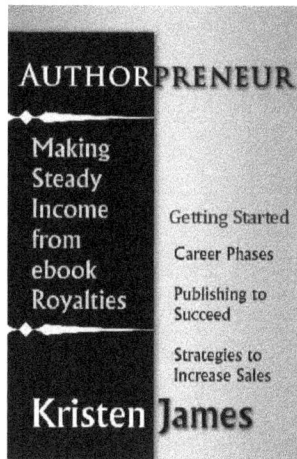

Authorpreneur: Making Steady Income from Ebook Royalties

New 2015 International Edition

Authorpreneur: a noun. A professional author/entrepreneur who strives to improve in all areas of the publishing business: writing, publishing and marketing.

What does it really take to make it as an author? What are realistic production and promotion costs? Do many people make money publishing ebooks, and how much?

"Authorpreneur" takes a look at what's involved in independent publishing and what you can expect at different career phases such as:

Starting Out with ebook publishing

Multi-published author

Earning $500 per month and growing

And even feeling stuck in writing and marketing

I discuss real numbers and what success means to different people—it's not just about money. This book is for writers who value great storytelling and connecting with readers, and who want to develop their career, not just spike ebook sales for a month.

"Authorpreneur" is filled with tips you can do during set up, how to get sales moving again, and all the strategies I've used to sell more books, doubling my sales every year and tripling my income.